MW01616634

ABIDING IN THE
FATHER'S LOVE

BY
JOE MCINTYRE

ABIDING IN THE FATHER'S LOVE

Published by
Empowering Grace Ministries
18706 N. Creek Pkwy., Suite 104
Bothell, WA 98011
Email: *joe_mcintyre@msn.com*

Capitalization: Joe McIntyre has taken *Author's Prerogative* in capitalizing certain words that are not usually capitalized according to standard grammatical practice. This is done for the purpose of clarity and emphasis.

Unless otherwise noted, all Scripture quotations are from the New King James Version of the Bible. Copyright © 1979, 1980, 1982 by Thomas Nelson Inc., publishers. Used by permission.

ISBN: 978-0-9778338-3-2

Printed in the United States by Morris Publishing
3212 East Highway 30
Kearney, NE 68847
1-800-650-7888

DEDICATION

I want to dedicate this book to the little girl on the cover of this book, my daughter, Torie McIntyre. She's grown a little since this picture was taken. My daughter has just graduated from college with honors. Torie, I love you and am very proud of you. If our Heavenly Father delights in us as much as my heart delights in you, we are all richly blessed.

ACKNOWLEDGEMENTS

Linda Boone, our Church Administrator and my Personal Assistant has been invaluable in preparing my books for publishing. Thank you, Linda. My wife Pam has been a wonderful encouragement to me to keep me writing and actually finishing books! Thanks also to Sue Costello for her help on preparing the manuscript. May Ridaliste has once again done a great job on the cover. Marilyn Ratto once again offered her services in editing the book. Thank you, Marilyn. Word of His Grace Church and Ministry Center has been wonderfully supportive and our leadership team has shared much responsibility in overseeing the Body allowing me the necessary time to write. Thanks so much.

CONTENTS

FOREWORD

God's plan is for blessings to flow from generation to generation. A father's blessing is the impartation of identity and destiny through words, actions and touch.

Our Heavenly Father is calling us to intimate fellowship with Himself. After 16 years of living the Christian life, I had never experienced the depths of Daddy-God's love for me. In the year 2000, my life was radically transformed as I experienced a baptism of love, and my service was no longer on the basis of my acceptance, nor the purpose for my redemption. It is the fruit of my love relationship and intimacy with the Father. Father God's supernatural love displaced fear, rejection, and addiction. I discovered I was a beloved son who my Father loves and that He is well pleased with me.

Prodigal sons and daughters are returning home. They are coming home to a compassionate and forgiving Father. Fathers and mothers have begun to be humbled by God's love and are asking forgiveness from their children for misrepresenting God's love to them (Malachi 4:5-6; Luke 15:17-24).

This very timely book "Abiding in the Father's Love" is a powerful introduction to one of the most important end times agenda: "Restoring the hearts of the fathers to the children, and the hearts of the children to the fathers" (Malachi 4:4-6).

The foundation of our spiritual inheritance in the Kingdom of God can be found in every page of this book as sons and daughters receive revelation of the Father's love.

Read this book and proceed slowly and cautiously! If there are statements which call for questions, pause and ponder before going on. Where scripture and references are given, take time to read and then meditate on them. My friend, Joe, will lead you on a journey to Father God that will say, "For I know the thoughts I think toward you, saith the LORD, thoughts of peace, and not of evil, to give you an expected end" (Jeremiah 29:11).

May His Holy Spirit cause you to see yourself through the Father's loving eyes as beloved sons and daughters.

Leif Hetland

President
Global Mission Awareness
Author Souring As Eagles

ENDORSEMENTS

Joe McIntyre has one of the clearest messages on the Father's heart of anyone I know. I have been greatly impacted through his ministry, both is his preaching and his writing. And now he gives us Abiding in the Father's Love. This is a wonderful book filled with insights and grace that are sure to powerfully impact all who read it.

Bill Johnson

Senior Pastor of Bethel Church, Redding, CA

INTRODUCTION

The Father of Lights, with Whom there is no shadow of turning, invites you into deep, rich fellowship with Him. You were created for this. Your life will never know the security and significance for which you were brought forth without the experience of your Father's love for you.

Our walk with the Lord is hindered to the degree that we fall short of entering into the place of loving acceptance prepared for us in Jesus Christ. We end up striving for approval instead of basking in our God-given standing in grace. We work hard instead of trusting much. We wear ourselves out trying to please a Father we're not sure accepts us, when He has made every provision for our complete acceptance now.

This book beckons you to learn to receive your Father's love. Father has prepared a place of rest for you. Only you can fill that place. If you don't fill it, it will remain unfilled because it was created for you alone. Your Father grieves when you struggle and strive to find worthiness before Him when He placed you in Christ where there is no condemnation.

Many are concerned with the amount of sin in the Church. They are contending for a revival of repentance. Sometimes, however, these attempts are misguided. When Jesus spoke of the Holy Spirit coming to convict of sin, He only mentions one particular sin.

John 16:8-9

And when He has come, He will convict the world of sin, and of righteousness, and of judgment: of **sin**, because **they do not believe in Me**.

The sin that the Holy Spirit comes to convict men of is unbelief. This is the root of every other sin. This doesn't apply only to the lost. What Jesus has done for us, we only partially apprehend when we are Born Again. Jesus has accomplished a perfect work that meets every need of mankind. He now ever lives to intercede for us and is able to bring us to full salvation. He has opened up a new and living way into the presence and fellowship of the Father. It is not related to how sanctified we are but is available to the youngest new believer. It doesn't depend on how holy our works are, but how holy His work is.

The real key to lasting change is beholding the glory of God in the face of Jesus Christ. The Father drew us to the Son and revealed Him to us. You could not have come to Jesus unless the Father had drawn you. Now the Son desires to reveal the Father to you. He has opened the Way by His blood, for you to draw near with confidence. We grow in faith as our fellowship deepens with the Father. To know Him is to love Him. To love Him is to trust Him. To trust Him is to believe His Word.

The purpose of this book is to stir up your hunger to know the Father. Deep within all of us is a longing that can't be satisfied with anything else except the knowledge of Him. The good news is that this longing is not one-sided. He longs to know you intimately as well. He created you for this relationship and fellowship. He won't be satisfied until you know Him and enter into the rest predestined for you. Out of that rest will flow everything the Father desires to see in your life.

-1-

THE ULTIMATE GOAL OF OUR FAITH

When I was a boy, I went to a religious school. We were taught to memorize many statements about God. These statements were often brought to us in question-and-answer form.

Why did God make us? Answer: *God made us to know, love and serve Him.*

One of the great causes of guilt and condemnation in the Church today is the lack of desire many have to serve God. They know they should want to serve Him, but don't find it in their hearts to give God their whole-hearted devotion. Could this be rooted in an image of God that is a distortion of the biblical picture of our Father? Many see God, not as a loving Father who longs for a deep relationship with us, but rather a just, austere, holy Being who is ever on the alert to show us our sin. Many think *if I could get a revelation of how sinful I am, maybe I would find lasting change.*

Certainly our Father wants us to walk in holiness. But is a deeper conviction of our sinfulness the key to lasting change? I want to suggest that the revelation we need is not one of our sinfulness. Rather, we need revelation of who He is and what He has provided for us in His Son. It is the *goodness* of God that leads us to repentance (Rom.2:4). We can't expect to love and serve a God whom we hardly know, or One we have greatly misunderstood.

The Revelation of the Father

Part of the problem we face is that the Father can only be known by revelation. Since He is an invisible spirit being, we can't "image" Him. Most of us, then, call to mind some image of Jesus we've seen. We often pray to Jesus, Whom we can imagine, and not to the Father, Whom we can't imagine.

There seems to be a pattern in the unfolding of the various members of the Godhead. First, the Father draws us to Jesus.

John 6:65
And He said, "Therefore I have said to you that no one can come to Me unless it has been granted to him by My Father."

If we have come to know Jesus as our Lord and Savior, it is because the Father drew us to Him and revealed Him to us. When Jesus asked His disciples who men said He was, the disciples gave various answers. When He asked them who they believed He was, Peter said, "You are the Christ, the Son of the Living God" (Mt. 16:16). Jesus, recognizing that Peter spoke from revelation commented, "Flesh and blood has not revealed this to you, but My Father which is in heaven" (Mt. 16:17).

Matthew 11:27

All things have been delivered to Me by My Father, and no one knows the Son except the Father. Nor does anyone know the Father except the Son, and the one to whom the Son wills to reveal Him.

In this passage we see that no one knows the Son except the Father. Comparing that with the previous passage we see that the revelation of the Son is given only by the Father. But then Jesus goes on to point out that no one knows the Father except the Son and the one to whom the Son reveals Him. So part of the ministry of Jesus is to reveal to us the Father.

The Protestant Reformation

The Protestant Reformation was actually birthed because Martin Luther had the Father revealed to him by Jesus. We see this in the following quote from Luther. He had been meditating on Romans 1:17.

This passage of Paul became to me a gate of heaven... If you have a true faith that Christ is your Savior, then at once you have a gracious God, for faith leads you in and opens up God's heart and will, that you should see pure grace and overflowing love. This it is to behold God in faith, that you should look upon His Fatherly, friendly heart, in which there is no anger nor ungraciousness. He who sees God as angry does not see

Him rightly, but looks only on a curtain, as if a dark cloud had been drawn across His face. [1]

The Reformation began with a revelation of the nature of the Father that revolutionized Luther's life. His image of God the Father was healed and his love for God was quickened by this revelation. Many of those who followed Luther, faithfully preached justification by faith as a doctrine, but didn't capture the effect that this truth was supposed to have on our image of God the Father. It was this revelation that transformed Luther. And this revelation still transforms those who receive it today.

The Ministry of Jesus

Jesus greatly desires to bring us into a deep, life-transforming revelation of His Father.

John 14:6

Jesus said to him, "I am the way, the truth, and the life. No one comes to the Father except through Me."

An often overlooked aspect of the ministry of Jesus is His obsession with revealing His Father. He is the perfect revelation of the Father. He is the Father revealed. "If you've seen Me, you've seen the Father," He said (Jn. 14:9). We can't get a full understanding of Who the Father is looking at in the Old Testament. He is only partially revealed there. But in Christ, we see the Father fully disclosed.

---

[1] *Here I Stand*, Roland Bainton, 50.

Heb 1:1-3 Holman Christian Standard Bible

Long ago God spoke to the fathers by the prophets at different times and in different ways. In these last days, He has spoken to us by *His* Son, whom He has appointed heir of all things and through whom He made the universe. He is the radiance of His glory, the exact expression of His nature, and He sustains all things by His powerful word. After making purification for sins, He sat down at the right hand of the Majesty on high.

The Father has spoken His final Word in His Son. He is the radiance of His glory and the exact expression of His nature. "If you've seen Me, you've seen My Father." Jesus has come to reveal His Father and bring us into a powerful encounter with Him.

John 1:18 AMP

No man has ever seen God at any time; *the only unique Son,* The only-begotten God, Who is in the bosom [in the intimate presence] of the Father, He has declared Him [He has revealed Him, **brought Him out where He can be seen;** He has interpreted Him and He has made Him known].

The Father is Seeking You

All of your life, whether you knew it or not, the Father has been seeking you. He has chosen you before time began and given you purpose and grace (2 Tim. 1:9). The Fall made us fear God and His holiness. Grace calls us to walk with Him and delivers us from our fears. He gives us His righteousness and His holiness in the New Creation.

Ephesians 4:24

...and that you put on the new man which was created according to God, in true righteousness and holiness.

At the essence of your being you have been made new. You are His workmanship and He likes what He makes. Old things have passed away. All things have become new. And all things are of God (2 Cor. 5:17-18). Dare to believe He has solved the unworthiness problem. He is your worthiness.

He did this because He wants you in relationship with Him. He has removed every barrier between Himself and His creation. How He must grieve when He sees us struggling to become acceptable to Him. It must break His heart. *If they would only believe what I've done for them, they would be full of joy and gladness.*

John 4:24 The Message

God is sheer being itself - Spirit. Those who worship him must do it out of their very being, their spirits, their true selves, in adoration.

In this brilliant paraphrase, our likeness to God in spirit - our true selves - is pointed to as the part of us that knows and worships God. Our human spirit was cut off from God due to the Fall, but in Christ we have been made alive in spirit and our spirits long to connect with our Father. Our Father put this hunger in us so He could fulfill it and please His own heart.

Eph 1:3-7 RSV

Blessed be the God and Father of our Lord Jesus Christ, who has blessed us in Christ with every spiritual blessing in the heavenly places, even as he chose us in him before the foundation of the world, that we should be holy and blameless before him. He destined us in love to be his sons through Jesus Christ, according to the purpose of his will, to the praise of his glorious grace which he freely bestowed on us in the Beloved.

In this amazing passage, we see the heart of our Father purposing in Christ to have us in relationship with Him before the world was. We were destined to be His sons. We are not the servants of God. A son may serve his father, but he does it in a different spirit than a servant. He does it as partner in the family business. We are partners in our Father's business. It's called the kingdom of God.

Ephesians 2:4-10

But God, who is rich in mercy, because of His great love with which He loved us, even when we were dead in trespasses, made us alive together with Christ (by grace you have been saved), and raised us up together, and made us sit together in the heavenly places in Christ Jesus, that in the ages to come He might show the exceeding riches of His grace in His kindness toward us in Christ Jesus. For by grace you have been saved through faith, and that not of yourselves; it is the gift of God, not of works, lest anyone should boast. For we are His workmanship, created in Christ Jesus for good works, which God prepared beforehand that we should walk in them.

Compelled by the richness of His heart of mercy and the great love He had toward us, even when we were still lost and in rebellion, He has made us alive with Christ. He has given us New Life in His Son and we are now seated with Christ actually, enthroned in the heavenlies. We are His workmanship having been recreated through our union with Christ in spirit. We are created for a God-chosen destiny that Father designed that will cause us to be filled with joy as we press on to discover it.

Many believers are haunted by the ghost of the Old Man. They are focused on trying to kill the old life in Adam. As a New Creation in Christ, the Old Man is gone. You may still have mental and emotional strongholds that need to be pulled down and put out of your life, but these strongholds are not the real you. The Devil says these continuing problem areas prove you haven't died to the old life and you need to focus on dying more.

Has God Said?

Just like the serpent in the Garden, Satan challenges the Word of God. The Word says you *were* crucified with Christ, died with Him and were buried with Him. All the verbs in the original language are past tense.[2] It's not a process, as some have suggested, but an event. An event that took place on the cross, and in Christ's death and subsequent resurrection. You don't have to make this happen, God made it happen. You have only to believe it and receive it. It is God's gift to you.

---

[2] The verbs dealing with our joint death, burial and resurrection are either aorist (once and for all) or perfect (done with continuing results).

19

When it dawns on us all that the Father has done to make us acceptable to Him, we begin to see that His love for us must be amazing. Why else would He go to so much effort to make a way for us to confidently approach Him? The consuming fire of His love burns for us and calls us to come and fellowship with Him.

Men's traditions and Satan's deceptions have conspired to hide this call to experience Father's love. Since the Father must be known by revelation, we are somewhat hindered initially in our understanding of who the Father is. E.W. Kenyon observed;

> Satan has been very subtle in blinding our minds to the Father-nature of God. The average Christian has had no real consciousness of God as being his Father. Man's mind derives its knowledge through the senses of the physical body. The Father has never been manifested to these senses, as He is a Spirit being, therefore man's mind can form no mental picture of Him.

> When a man has been born again, past Sense Knowledge of the life of Jesus Christ has taken the place that the Father should have had in his life. Because man could form a mental image of Christ, he has developed the habit of praying to Christ, praising and worshipping Him alone. The renewing of man's mind by the Word of God brings a consciousness of the Father to him that revolutionizes his life. [3]

---

[3] *Basic Bible Study Course,* E.W. Kenyon, Lesson One, p. 7.

A Strong Faith Life

Fellowship with the Father establishes us in the grace of God. It opens up the Word to us and it becomes the voice of God to us. Our Father speaks personally to us through His promises and the statements of truth in the Word. Our faith life begins to blossom like never before. Condemnation is uprooted and we refuse the subtle accusations of the enemy. We know our Father loves us. As Luther noted, we see the Fatherly, friendly heart of God in which there is no anger or ungraciousness. This is how faith beholds the Father.

The Word says, "Faith comes by hearing, hearing by the Word of God," (Rom. 10:17). But an important question to ask is, "Where does faith come from?" I believe the right answer is *faith comes from the heart of the Father through the Word of God to our hearts.* As our faith in God's love for us grows, His Word becomes His voice directly to our hearts. No longer is the Word just letters on a page, but it becomes the Living Voice of Heaven to our hearts. A joyful faith is imparted to us as we learn to quietly meditate in the promises of God. The Holy Spirit quickens the Word and it begins to live in our hearts. The promises of Scripture become our Father's promises to us. We claim them as our own.

Since, without faith it is impossible to please God, we find our deepening fellowship with the Father is producing a greater impartation from the Word. Our faith grows exceedingly. The written Word is becoming for us the Living Word. Christ Himself is being revealed and imparted to us through the channel of the written Word. Our ability to totally trust in the faithfulness of God develops marvelously. Our peace and joy increase accordingly.

Paul told us that what is important in the Christian life is "faith working by love" (Gal. 5:6). He may have been telling us that real faith leads to a walk in Christian love. Or he could have been saying that our faith lacks its essence when we don't know the love of God for us. His love for us undergirds our faith walk and gives it its foundation. As we come to know we are loved, it becomes much easier to trust the Father and His Word. As E.W. Kenyon has stated: "Fellowship is the parent of Real Faith. If you find someone whose Faith is weak, you may know that his fellowship has been broken or is of a low type." [4]

Father is calling us to join His army of Father-Pleasers. Son number One is leading the Way. As we enter into this deeper, richer fellowship with Him, His passion burns in our hearts. We want what He wants. The consuming fire of His love begins to possess us and we begin to 'spread the fire.' In order to appreciate His fiery love, we must have an accurate view of why man was created. We will examine this in the next chapter.

---

[4] *In His Presence,* E.W. Kenyon, p. 86.

-2-

MAN: THE REASON FOR CREATION

In Father's original plan for Man we see His heart revealed. He created us to walk with Him in fellowship and to rule on His behalf. His purpose has not changed. We must always remember: God's work in Christ is vastly superior to Satan's work in Adam. To fully appreciate the New Creation, we must see accurately the original purpose of God for Man.

Genesis 1:26-28
Then God said, "Let Us make man in Our image, according to Our likeness; let them have dominion over the fish of the sea, over the birds of the air, and over the cattle, over all the earth and over every creeping thing that creeps on the earth." So God created man in His own image; in the image of God He created him; male and female He created them. Then God blessed them, and God said to them, "Be fruitful and multiply; fill the earth and subdue it; have dominion over the fish of the sea, over the birds of the air, and over every living thing that moves on the earth."

Adam Was Created in the Image and Likeness of God

Father created us in His image. The Bible Knowledge Commentary notes "Being in God's image means humans share, though imperfectly and finitely, in God's nature, that is, in His communicable attributes - life, personality, truth, wisdom, love, holiness, justice - and so have the capacity for spiritual fellowship with Him."

In Christ, we see that Father is restoring this image:

> **Ephesians 4:23-24**
> ...and be renewed in the spirit of your mind, and that you put on the new man which was created according to God, in true righteousness and holiness.

As our minds are renewed to New Covenant Truth, we learn to walk in the righteousness and holiness already ours in Christ. Father took His own righteousness and holiness and brought forth a New Creation in each of us. We are His workmanship. The same Truth is brought out in Colossians:

> **Colossians 3:9-10**
> Do not lie to one another, since you have put off the old man with his deeds, and have put on the new man who *is renewed* in knowledge according to the image of Him who created him.

The verb in verse 10 (is renewed) is present tense and could be translated *is continually being renewed into precise knowledge.*

This renewal process began at the New Birth and continues until we are fully conformed to the image of God's Son.

Romans 8:29
For whom He foreknew, He also predestined to be conformed to the image of His Son, that He might be the firstborn among many brethren.

You are predestined, by Your Father's eternal purpose, to be conformed to the image of His Son. Jesus came with the two-fold purpose of revealing the Father and showing us what God intended Man to be like. Jesus is both Eternal Deity and Perfect Humanity revealed. Father's purpose is that He be the firstborn of many brethren. We cannot, of course, be Eternal Deity. But we can *reveal* Him who is Eternal Deity. The Perfect Humanity of the Son of God can be revealed in us as well. Don't put this off to some later age. You are in process now! Unbelief would limit God and say this must be after I die and go to heaven. Don't be like Israel, who limited their God. Be like Caleb and Joshua, whom God said were of a different spirit.

Man: Created for Dominion

Man was created and placed in an environment that had a hostile element: the serpent! When Father created Man He gave him dominion. The Hebrew word for dominion means, "to tread down, to subjugate."[5] Another source says, "to subject, to subdue, to force, to keep under, to bring into bondage." [6]

---

[5] Strong's Concordance.
[6] Brown, Driver, and Briggs Hebrew Lexicon.

Man was to be God's under ruler. His assignment was to subdue and rule over the serpent and his cohorts. Having failed initially, Father has restored him and given him authority to accomplish this task again.

> **Romans 16:20**
> And the God of peace will crush Satan under your feet shortly. The grace of our Lord Jesus Christ be with you. Amen.

As we come together in unity, we are enabled to corporately crush Satan under our feet. Individually, in our sphere of responsibility, we also have this authority. It is restored to us in Christ. Created for dominion, dominion is restored to us through Christ's Finished Work. Father calls us to walk in this authority.

Adam's Mind Was Extremely Capable

In the original Creation, Adam's mind was very capable. Notice what the Word says about his abilities as created by Father:

> **Genesis 2:20**
> So Adam gave names to all cattle, to the birds of the air, and to every beast of the field.

Adam named all the animals! Think of how many different types and species of animals there are. Yet Adam could name and remember them all! His mind and memory must have been enormously capable. We are told today that Man only uses 15% of his mental faculties. Is it possible that when Man fell, he lost access to his own spirit's abilities and this affected his intellectual abilities? I think this is a distinct possibility.

But now our spirits have been made alive with Christ. What does this do (at least potentially) for our minds? I think it opens up great possibilities. As Paul noted;

> **1 Corinthians 2:16**
> For "who has known the mind of the Lord that he may instruct Him?" But we have the mind of Christ.

Paul indicated that the apostolic team (and potentially all believers) were operating in the mind of Christ. Could this now be resident in your spirit by the Holy Spirit's indwelling? Could we learn to access the mind of Christ within us and learn to govern our lives by this mind? Paul certainly implies this possibility.

Adam Walked with Father

Adam met regularly with God. He had fellowship with Him. He was at home in the Father's presence. Actually, as the Hebrew says, *before His face*. Before the face of the God of the universe, Adam felt accepted and at home.

> **Genesis 2:25**
> And they were both naked, the man and his wife, and were not ashamed.

Before they fell, Adam and Eve had no shame. But when sin entered, the face of God was now fearful and they retreated from Father God.

Genesis 3:8
And they heard the sound of the Lord God walking in the garden in the cool of the day, and Adam and his wife hid themselves from the presence [face] of the Lord God among the trees of the garden.

In this revealing passage, we find that sin caused Adam and his wife to hide from the Face of God. Apparently, Father manifested Himself to them in a form in which they could behold His Face. And it was normal to stand before His Face unashamed and have fellowship with Him. Normally, they would hear the sound (or voice) of the Father calling them to come before His Face and have fellowship with Him. Out of this fellowship they would likely receive His counsel on how to implement the dominion assignment.

But sin entered and condemnation and shame robbed Man of his glorious privilege. We need to see that sin also robbed our Father of His delight in His fellowship with Man – this Man, whom He had created for the purpose of fellowship with Himself. How it must have grieved His heart when His Man drew back from Him and feared to come before His Face.

In Christ, we are called back to behold the Face of the Father as it is revealed in Christ.

2 Corinthians 4:6

For it is the God who commanded light to shine out of darkness, who has shone in our hearts to give the light of the knowledge of the glory of God in the face of Jesus Christ.

As we learn by the Spirit to behold the Face of Christ, we are changed into the same image.

2 Corinthians 3:18

But we all, with unveiled face, beholding as in a mirror the glory of the Lord, are being transformed into the same image from glory to glory, just as by the Spirit of the Lord.

As we are drawn into an intimate fellowship with the Father and the Son, we 'behold' the glory of God in the Face of Jesus Christ. This unveiling to our hearts causes us to be changed into the same image. Seeing His resurrection glory we are transformed. As we are transformed, our minds are renewed and the world's patterns drop off of our lives.

Romans 12:2

And do not be conformed to this world, but be transformed by the renewing of your mind, that you may prove what is that good and acceptable and perfect will of God.

As our minds are renewed to our acceptance in the presence of God - our welcome before His Face - we lose our conformity to the world and this age. We taste the powers of the age to come and learn to live in its realities while still walking in this age.

Galatians 1:4

who gave Himself for our sins, that He might deliver us from this present evil age, according to the will of our God and Father.

It is the Father's will that we walk free from the downward pull of this present age. As we behold Him we are changed and our minds become renewed to the reality that this age has no authority over us. The Kingdom comes in us and the will of God is done through us. Our renewed minds receive the Truth that we are created to fellowship with the Father through the revelation of the glory of Christ. Our longed for transformation is now being appropriated as we enjoy a deep, rich fellowship with the Father.

Man Was Created to Eat of the Tree of Life

Genesis 2:8-9

The Lord God planted a garden eastward in Eden, and there He put the man whom He had formed. And out of the ground the Lord God made every tree grow that is pleasant to the sight and good for food. The tree of life was also in the midst of the garden, and the tree of the knowledge of good and evil.

Man was created to eat of Christ: the Tree of Life. Now, restored to the Father in Christ, we can eat of the Living Word. Every spiritual blessing is now ours in Christ (Eph. 1:3). The faith that is now ours is overcoming the world (1 Jn. 5:4) and the Tree of Life is now ours to enjoy.

Revelation 2:7

He who has an ear, let him hear what the Spirit says to the churches. To him who overcomes I will give to eat from the tree of life, which is in the midst of the Paradise of God.

Access to the Paradise of His Presence has been granted us. This means we can eat of the Tree of Life. As we enjoy this we become a treasure to the heart of God. We will discuss this in the next chapter.

-3-

FATHER'S SPECIAL TREASURE

Numbers 14:8-9

If the Lord delights in us, then He will bring us into this land and give it to us 'a land which flows with milk and honey.' Only do not rebel against the Lord, nor fear the people of the land, for they are our bread; their protection has departed from them, and the Lord is with us. Do not fear them.

In the passage above, Caleb and Joshua have just returned from spying out the Land of Canaan. The twelve spies went in at the direction of the Lord to see if it was, indeed, a land flowing with milk and honey. They were not sent to see if they thought they could take the Land. God had already told them that He had given them the Land.

Ten of the spies came back with an evil report. What they saw caused them to disregard the Word of the Lord and move into fear. God said that Caleb, however, had a different spirit. Notice the key to this different spirit: "If the Lord delights in us..." Caleb and Joshua dared to believe that God delighted in them!

Remember, this is under the Old Covenant. These are not Born Again men who have the Spirit of God dwelling in them. Yet their faith in God is so strong that the revelation of God's goodness has swallowed up their consciousness of sin and unworthiness. How much more may we New Covenant believers dare to trust in the power of the Blood of Jesus to utterly cleanse us and make us fit to stand in the presence of the Father.

Ask yourself the question, *Do I know that God delights in me?* If you are somewhat uncertain about this knowledge, then the good news is that the Father wants you to become certain. He wants to establish your heart in grace (Heb. 13:9).

The Eternal Purpose of God

When the Father created us it was to fulfill the desire of His own heart. He wanted a people. After the Fall His purpose was delayed but not changed. He wanted a people for Himself. Observe the calling of Israel:

> **Exodus 19:5-6**
> Now therefore, if you will indeed obey My voice and keep My covenant, then you shall be **a special treasure to Me** above all people; for all the earth is Mine. And you shall be to Me a kingdom of priests and a holy nation. These are the words which you shall speak to the children of Israel.

Father was looking for a people for Himself. Not just to obey Him, though obedience was a key to staying in right standing. But He wanted a people to have a relationship with and to whom He could reveal Himself. Through this company who were His special treasure He would reveal Himself to the surrounding nations.

The Hebrew word for 'special treasure' means *a private possession one personally acquires and carefully preserves.*[7] Our Father is looking for a people that are entirely His. He wants a company of sons who have the heart of Son Number One, a company of Father-Pleasers.

God's Heart

We catch glimpses of Father's heart hunger throughout the Old Covenant.

> **Deuteronomy 5:29**
>
> Oh, that they had such a heart in them that they would fear Me and always keep all My commandments, that it might be well with them and with their children forever!

The Father's heart longs for a people He can bless without violating the principles of His holy Covenant. In the Old Covenant their standing was based on their outward obedience to the commandments. When they failed, they had a sacrificial system that provided forgiveness and the removal of the sin. People were capable of walking in right standing under the Old Covenant. Many did.

But the key was their faith in God, not the perfection of their obedience. Many great Old Covenant figures had awful failures in their lives. But because their hearts were after God and they came to Him with their sin, they found forgiveness and

---

[7] Vine's Expository Dictionary of Biblical Words.

continued in relationship with God. He called them His friends. If such a relationship was possible under the Old Covenant, how much more should we expect to find it under the New.

God wanted Israel to be His special treasure. He kept giving voice to His desire:

> **Deuteronomy 7:6**
> For you are a holy people to the Lord your God; the Lord your God has chosen you to be **a people for Himself, a special treasure** above all the peoples on the face of the earth.

There are many facets to the purpose of the Father for His people. The most basic and foundational is His desire for a family, a people for Himself. Let this saying sink deep in your ears: Your Father wants to know you intimately and for you to know Him in the same manner. This is why you were created. Everything else is secondary. This is the glue that will hold everything together. This is the foundation upon which everything is built. This truth will hold you steady when the world around you is shaking.

The first generation of Israel that came out of Egypt never became what the Father desired. So He continued His quest with the next generation.

> **Deuteronomy 26:17-19**
> Today you have proclaimed the Lord to be your God, and that you will walk in His ways and keep His statutes, His commandments, and His judgments, and that you will obey

His voice. Also today the Lord has proclaimed you to be **His special people**, just as He promised you, that you should keep all His commandments, and that He will set you high above all nations which He has made, in praise, in name, and in honor, and that you may be a holy people to the Lord your God, just as He has spoken.

As the second generation prepared to enter the Promised Land they proclaimed the Lord to be their God. These words in the Hebrew are interesting. Gesenius Hebrew-Chaldee Lexicon notes that the meaning is "you have this day made the Lord to say, or promise," verse 18, "and the Lord has made you promise, i.e., you have mutually promised, and accepted, and ratified the conditions of each other."[8]

The faith of that second generation caused the Lord to covenant with them to be their God and they would be His special treasure. He promised to set them on high above all the nations.

We have a better covenant based on better promises!

Looking Forward

Even the generations that entered the Land ultimately failed Him. At the close of the Old Covenant, Malachi prophesied of a people who feared the Lord and spoke to one another in that spirit of reverence.

---

[8] Genesius Hebrew-Chaldee Lexicon. p. 61.

36

Malachi 3:16-18

Then those who feared the Lord spoke to one another, and the Lord listened and heard them; So a book of remembrance was written before Him for those who fear the Lord, And who meditate on His name. "They shall **be Mine**," says the Lord of hosts, "On the day that **I make them My jewels.** And I will spare them as a man spares his own son who serves him." Then you shall again discern between the righteous and the wicked, between one who serves God and one who does not serve Him.

Father God's determination to have a people who are His "jewels" is expressed here. The word translated *jewels* is the same word translated *special treasure* elsewhere. This desire of God's is the heartbeat of His purpose. His love for the world cannot be fully expressed until He finds a people for His own possession. Jesus expressed it this way:

John 17:21

...that they all may be one, as You, Father, are in Me, and I in You; that they also may be one in Us, that the world may believe that You sent Me.

Father God is bringing forth a people whose union with Christ parallels Christ's union with the Father. When this people come forth it will cause the world to believe that God sent Jesus. This is another way of speaking of His special treasure.

The apostle Paul captures this idea beautifully in his letter to Titus:

Titus 2:14

who gave Himself for us, that He might redeem us from every lawless deed and purify **for Himself His own special people**, zealous for good works.

The ultimate means of finally having this people who are His special treasure was to give His only Son to redeem us to Himself. In the Old Covenant, when Israel gave themselves to the Lord, it motivated Him to give Himself to them. In the New Covenant the Father gives Jesus to us first and our response is to give ourselves to Him freely. We are to abandon our hearts to Him in loving trust.

In the glorious realities of the New Covenant we have become the very thing the Father has wanted all along. But so many of us have not even understood the privilege we have in Christ. Peter tells us the good news:

1 Peter 2:9-10

But you are a chosen generation, a royal priesthood, a holy nation, **His own special people**, that you may proclaim the praises of Him who called you out of darkness into His marvelous light; who once were not a people but are now the people of God, who had not obtained mercy but now have obtained mercy.

We are God's special treasure, the desire of His heart. He delights in us. In Christ we are everything He wants us to be. We can come with boldness to His throne of grace. Father has opened up a New and Living Way through His Son and His Son's blood.

Dare to believe it!

-4-

THE HEART OF THE MATTER

It is important that even with our limited capacity to comprehend it, we seek to understand God's perspective on the Fall of Man. The Father's dream for a Family of sons and daughters who walked with Him and did His will was disrupted and derailed. I understand that nothing catches God by surprise, but God's Father-Heart was certainly moved by the great tragedy of sin entering the world of man.

Fear, shame and condemnation began to dominate the species of Man. Instead of enjoying God's presence, man began to fear His presence. Over time, darkness overtook man's consciousness and his perception of spiritual things was for the most part lost.

> **Ephesians 4:17-18**
> This I say, therefore, and testify in the Lord, that you should no longer walk as the rest of the Gentiles walk, in the futility of their mind, having their understanding darkened, being alienated from the life of God, because of the ignorance that is in them, because of the blindness of their heart;

In this passage, Paul exhorts believers to refrain from walking as the unsaved do. Their understanding, he says, is darkened because they are alienated from the Life of God. The darkness-

40

dominated heart of the unbeliever is the problem. This is what God faced in fallen man. Notice what is said right before the flood:

Genesis 6:5-6

Then the Lord saw that the wickedness of man was great in the earth, and that **every intent of the thoughts of his heart was only evil continually.** And the Lord was sorry that He had made man on the earth, and He was grieved in His heart.

The hearts of fallen men were given over to darkness. Clearly their hearts were hardened against the influences of the Holy Spirit. This led to the judgment of the Flood. The darkened heart of man was the big obstacle to walking with the Father.

Even after Israel had been delivered from Egypt and had become the Covenant people of God, this problem continued.

Deuteronomy 5:29

Oh, that they had **such a heart in them** that they would fear Me and always keep all My commandments, that it might be well with them and with their children forever!

Here we see God's longing for man to have such a heart that He could bless them and they would deeply reverence Him. This evil would be portrayed in the Scriptures as an uncircumcised heart.

Deuteronomy 10:15-16

The Lord delighted only in your fathers, to love them; and He chose their descendants after them, you above all peoples, as it is this day. Therefore **circumcise the foreskin of your heart**, and be stiff-necked no longer.

Deuteronomy 30:6

And the Lord your God will **circumcise your heart** and the heart of your descendants, to love the Lord your God with all your heart and with all your soul, that you may live.

The human heart that is not pleasing to God is referred to as stiff-necked. In other words, slow to obey and self-willed. But God promises to ultimately circumcise the hearts of His people. It was this condition of the heart that kept the Father from drawing near His own Covenant people.

A Promised Answer

God began to sow hope into the hearts of His people while they were still in the wilderness. He promised to circumcise their hearts. He fully accomplished this through the Finished Work of Christ.

Romans 2:29

…but he is a Jew who is one inwardly; and circumcision is that of the heart, in the spirit, not in the letter; whose praise is not from men but from God.

Paul here refers to the true, spiritual circumcision. It has to do with the heart, not the body. It's more about breaking the dominion of the body over Man's being than fulfilling a religious obligation.

Colossians 2:11
In Him you were also circumcised with the circumcision made without hands, by putting off the body of the sins of the flesh, by the circumcision of Christ.

In this "spiritual" circumcision, the dominion of the flesh is broken over the inward man. What is "cut off" is the body's ability to control the renewed man. He is not under obligation to walk after the flesh any longer.

Philippians 3:3
For we are the circumcision, who worship God in the Spirit, rejoice in Christ Jesus, and have no confidence in the flesh.

Notice that the circumcision that Paul acknowledges is inward and spiritual and opposed to outward and physical. God had promised, and we have now received, if we are Born Again, this heart circumcision. Renew your mind and accept what Father has done for you.

A Heart of Flesh

Another way of referring to Man's heart problem was to liken it to the stone tablets on which the commandments were written.

At a time when Israel was deep in sin and in a backslidden condition, God promises to fix this heart problem.

> **Jeremiah 24:7**
> Then I will give them **a heart to know Me,** that I am the Lord; and **they shall be My people, and I will be their God,** for they shall return to Me with their whole heart.

This promise is one the greatest promises in the Old Covenant. God promises to put in us a heart to know Him. Father is looking for a people of whom it may be said that they are His people and He is their God. We can bring this promise before God's throne every day and ask Him to increase our knowledge of Him. Later, Jeremiah gives us more of God's heart and promise:

> **Jeremiah 31:33-34**
> But this is the covenant that I will make with the house of Israel after those days, says the Lord: I will put My law in their minds, and write it on their hearts; and **I will be their God, and they shall be My people.** No more shall every man teach his neighbor, and every man his brother, saying, 'Know the Lord,' for **they all shall know Me, from the least of them to the greatest of them,** says the Lord. For I will forgive their iniquity, and their sin I will remember no more.

In preparing the way for the New Covenant, Jeremiah tells us that it is God's intent that "all shall know Me." He goes on to say that what will make this possible is the fact that He will forgive their iniquity and forget their sins. He is going to offer them a "clean slate" in the matter of their hearts. This heart cleansing will open the door to a true knowledge of God. This is part of His plan to bring forth a people for Himself.

> **Ezekiel 11:19-20**
> Then I will give them **one heart**, and I will put **a new spirit** within them, and **take the stony heart out of their flesh**, and **give them a heart of flesh,** that they may walk in My statutes and keep My judgments and do them; and **they shall be My people, and I will be their God.**

God has promised to give to this prophesied people one heart and a new spirit. He will take out the stony heart and give them a tender heart upon which He can write His Instruction (the Hebrew word for *Law* means instruction). God Himself is going to solve the problem of Man's heart. He is going to deal with the condition in Man that hinders the kind of relationship the Father has always wanted with His sons and daughters. It is important enough that He mentions it again later in Ezekiel:

> **Ezekiel 36:26-28**
> I will give you **a new heart** and put **a new spirit** within you; I will take **the heart of stone out of your flesh** and give you **a heart of flesh. I will put My Spirit within you** and cause you to walk in My statutes, and you will keep My judgments and do them. Then you shall dwell in the land that I gave to your fathers; **you shall be My people, and I will be your God.**

Here we see an enlargement of the promise. *A new heart and a new spirit.* He will remove the stony heart and put in a heart of

45

flesh. He is then going to fill this renewed and cleansed inner man with the Holy Spirit.

A New Creation Heart

Paul, who was a great scholar of the Old Covenant, was given the task of showing how the New Covenant in Christ was the fulfillment of the Old Covenant. Sometimes, because of our lack of familiarity with the Old Covenant we can miss his references to it.

Corinth was a Church troubled by many internal problems. But notice how Paul refers to them in his second letter to them:

> **2 Corinthians 3:3 Recovery Version**
> Since you are being manifested that you are a letter of Christ ministered by us, inscribed not with ink but with the Spirit of the living God, not in tablets of stone, but in tablets of hearts of flesh.

The Corinthians, though still struggling with many fleshly issues, were reminded by Paul that they had received a new, cleansed heart. They were walking in what Paul in another letter refers to as the "futility of their minds" (Eph. 4:17). They weren't living out of the new heart they had received in the New Birth.

Many believers today, because of unbelief and a lack of good teaching, fail to appreciate what our Father has done for us in the New Birth. He has taken out the stony heart and given us a heart of flesh. He has given us a new spirit and put His Spirit within us. Put another way, He has solved the heart problem in Man that hindered Man's ability to fellowship with Him. Our great frustration when we do fail actually testifies to the fact that the new life in us hates the sin we commit. Someone has wisely said that the most miserable person on earth is not the unsaved who does not know anything but his present experience, but a believer who has known the peace of God and is currently living in sin.

The apostle Peter addresses this heart issue at the counsel in Jerusalem while discussing the Gentiles being accepted by the Jewish Christians.

Acts 15:7-9
And when there had been much dispute, Peter rose up and said to them: "Men and brethren, you know that a good while ago God chose among us, that by my mouth the Gentiles should hear the word of the gospel and believe. So God, who knows the heart, acknowledged them by giving them the Holy Spirit, just as He did to us, and made no distinction between us and them, **purifying their hearts by faith.**"

Peter here describes the effect of hearing and believing the gospel: the heart is purified by faith. So the only thing that can keep the sincere believer from rich fellowship with the Father is failing to believe what the Word says God has done for us. If we have no unconfessed sin in our lives, we may freely claim a pure heart before God. It was the Father's work and He does good work.

Someone will ask, "How can you say we have a clean heart, when we still fall into sin and disobedience?" To the degree that our minds remain unrenewed, we can still walk as unbelievers walk, in the futility of our minds. When mind and body rule over our spirits, we do the works of the flesh. Yet, all the time our deepest being is crying out for a walk in purity consistent with who we now are in Christ.

Avoiding Heart Problems

Many Christians today understand that we are justified by faith and not by works. But the Bible teaches that we are to live by faith. Faith is to be the lifestyle of the New Covenant believer. "Man", Jesus said, "shall not live by bread alone, but by every word that proceeds out of the mouth of God."

Our responsibility is to find out what God has said and then believe it with all of our hearts, regardless of any contrary indications. We are to protect our hearts from the faith-crippling disease called unbelief.

Hebrews 3:12
Beware, brethren, lest there be in any of you **an evil heart of unbelief** in departing from the living God...

Unbelief is the disease. Faith is the cure. Rich fellowship with the Father is the goal. Being fruitful is the result. You and I are called to "fight the good fight of faith" (1 Tim. 6:12). It's a good fight because the victory is already won! By faith we appropriate the victory over the adversary that Jesus has already won for us. Through faith and patience we inherit the promises (Heb. 6:12).

-5-

MY PEACE

John 14:27

Peace I leave with you, My peace I give to you; not as the world gives do I give to you. Let not your heart be troubled, neither let it be afraid.

Jesus walked and ministered from a platform of peace. He was resting in His spirit while doing amazing things in obedience to His Father. What was it that gave Jesus such great peace? How did He maintain it? How was this peace manifested? In this chapter, I want us to consider some lessons we can learn as we observe the walk of Jesus.

Jesus Knew He Was in Right Standing with His Father

As Jesus fulfilled His ministry, He enjoyed a sense of peace and well-being because He knew He was in right standing with His Father. There were no issues between Him and His Father that could hinder His fellowship. As we look at Jesus, we might say to ourselves, "Yes, but that was Jesus, He was sinless." It is true that He was sinless, but is the provision made by the Father in Christ's Finished Work sufficient to bring us into this same place of right standing? The answer is a glorious "yes!" What we could never attain by our performance becomes ours as a gift by faith.

Romans 4:25-5:2 Rutherford's Translation

…who was delivered up for our transgressions and was raised to make Righteousness possible for us. Once faith has brought us this Righteousness, we enjoy peace with God, through our Lord Jesus Christ, through whom we have also obtained our access to this state of grace in which we are and triumph in hope of attaining God's glory…

By believing that God raised Jesus from the dead, we are brought into perfect right standing with our Father. Through the work of His Son, our Father has made a way for us to come to Him just as though we had never sinned.

Romans 10:10

For with the heart one believes unto righteousness, and with the mouth confession is made unto salvation.

Right standing with the Father is a gift of His grace. He wanted us in right standing with Himself and paid the price of His Son to bring us into this standing in grace. The hand of faith receives what the grace of God freely offers. If you have believed that God raised Jesus from the dead, then you have believed unto righteousness.

Romans 5:17 Weymouth

For if, through the transgression of the one individual, Death made use of the one individual to seize the sovereignty, all the more shall those who receive God's overflowing grace and **gift of righteousness** reign as kings in Life through the one individual, Jesus Christ.

Overflowing grace and God's gift of righteousness bring us into a deep, rich fellowship with the Father out of which flows the strength and wisdom to reign in Life. You are one of God's kings and priests.

According to **1 Peter 2: 9 ESV**, "You are a chosen race, a royal priesthood, a holy nation, **a people for his own possession**, that you may proclaim the excellencies of him who called you out of darkness into his marvelous light."

Father has called us to walk and live in the Light of His countenance. In fact, He refers to us as light. "For you were once darkness, but **now you are light in the Lord**. Walk as children of light" (Ephesians 5:8). We were once in darkness but now we are the children of Light. As we learn to abide in the Light of His presence, we begin to show forth the Excellencies of the One who called us out of darkness into His Light.

> **1 John 1:7**
> But if we walk in the light as He is in the light, we have fellowship with one another, and the blood of Jesus Christ His Son cleanses us from all sin.

As long as we are seeking to walk uprightly in all the light we have, the blood continually cleanses us from all sin. If we are cleansed of all sin, certainly we are in right standing with our Father.

But sometimes we sin and disobey God. What does our Father want us to do if this happens?

1 John 1:9

If we confess our sins, He is faithful and just to forgive us our sins and to cleanse us from all unrighteousness.

While we are walking in broken fellowship, we have no access to the grace and forgiveness we need. We are out of agreement with heaven. But the remedy has been provided. We simply say to our Father, "Father, I have sinned. I am fully responsible for my wrong choices. I acknowledge my sin and I confess it to you. You said if I confess my sin You would be faithful and righteous to forgive me and cleanse me of all unrighteousness. Father I receive Your forgiveness and cleansing by faith, regardless of how I feel. You forgive me because of what Jesus did, not according to anything I deserve or merit. Because You forgive me I also choose to forgive myself. In Jesus' Name."

Without realizing it, believers operating in false, religious humility, fail to appropriate the cleansing power of the blood of Jesus. Father's intention is that you walk before Him with a conscience free from condemnation.

Hebrews 9:14

...how much more shall the blood of Christ, who through the eternal Spirit offered Himself without spot to God, cleanse your conscience from dead works to serve the living God?

For us to walk guilty and condemned is to unintentionally demean the power of the blood of Christ! In the New Covenant, in which God promises to remember your sins and lawless deeds no more, you can walk with a clean conscience (see Heb. 10:17). Through the overflowing grace of God you and I can walk in right standing with the Father just like Jesus did. It is a gift of grace, not a reward for holy living. Holy living is a fruit of the fellowship that grace makes possible. You stand before your Father as though sin had never been. You are as welcome in the presence of the Father as Jesus is.

Jesus Prioritized Fellowship with His Father

Jesus went off by Himself, sometimes through the whole night, to be in prayer and fellowship with His Father. Out of this intimacy He developed the hearing ear that always knew what the Father was doing in any given situation. This prayer intimacy, combined with the common Hebrew practice of Scripture meditation, enabled Jesus to do what He saw the Father doing and say what He heard the Father saying.

By faith we are to draw near to our Father in prayer.

Hebrews 10:19-22

Therefore, brethren, having boldness to enter the Holiest by the blood of Jesus, by a new and living way which He consecrated for us, through the veil, that is, His flesh, and having a High Priest over the house of God, let us draw near with a true heart in full assurance of faith, having our hearts sprinkled from an evil conscience and our bodies washed with pure water.

We boldly come into our Father's presence, trusting in Christ as our Surety, with a true (or honest) heart, having (already) sprinkled our hearts with the Blood of Jesus and obtaining a clean conscience, we approach our Father with the full assurance of faith.[9]

The only way we frail humans could have perfect right standing with the Father would be if He, in His mercy, made a provision for us and freely gave it to us. This is exactly what He has done! You are forgiven and in right standing with God. Thank Him for it! Praise Him for it. It's yours without working for it at all. Just receive it by faith and walk in it by grace.

To enjoy a victorious Christian life, we must, like Jesus, prioritize our fellowship with the Father. He has provided the way to come to Him. He is waiting for you to come. Come to Him now and bring Him the joy that issues from the work His Son accomplished on your behalf.

Jesus Lived to do His Father's Will

Psalms 40:7-8
Behold, I come; in the scroll of the book it is written of me. I delight to do Your will, O my God.

The entire focus of Jesus' ministry was doing His Father's will. As a Man, He was a willing vessel in the hands of His God. In the Father's purpose, Jesus is to be the Firstborn of many

---

[9] The Greek word translated *full assurance* means *fullness, firm conviction, absolute certainty.* Exegetical Dictionary of the New Testament.

brethren. You and I are to emulate Him. We are to be Father-Pleasers. As our minds are renewed, we progressively shed our selfish desires and bring ourselves by His grace into enlarging agreement with the Father's purpose and our foreordained destiny. We were chosen in Christ before the foundation of the earth to do good works that we grow into as our destiny unfolds.

The beginning place is a complete surrender to the will of the Father. By faith, recognizing that we need Him for this surrender to be effective, we choose to live for the will of God. We often fall short, but the Father is looking for the posture of our heart and its commitment to Him. Abraham was certainly shaky in His obedience but God honored the heart of Abraham that chose to obey and follow his God in faith. If it is the desire and passion of your heart to follow Him and do His will, your mistakes will not keep you from your destiny. Only your unbelief can cause you to miss God's purpose for your life. Some, in the irrationality of unbelief, have refused to submit all of their life to God and consequently have yet to find the place of fullness that Father has ordained for them.

Living to do the Father's will is another key to walking in the peace of God.

Jesus Did His Father's Works

Jesus frequently testified that the works He did were not His but His Father's.[10] The constant flow of the miraculous from the

---

[10] See, for example, John 5:30; 36-37; 6:38; 14:6-13

ministry of Jesus is an unveiling of the Father's heart toward broken humanity. Out of Jesus' right standing, intimacy in prayer and commitment to do His Father's will, flowed a river of healing and deliverance that shook the towns where He went. He was revealing the Father. Our ministry is to reveal this same Jesus who in turn will reveal His Father through us. Many think the works that Jesus did were because He was the Son of God, the Messiah. But note:

> **John 14:12-14**
>
> Most assuredly, I say to you, **he who believes in Me, the works that I do he will do also;** and greater works than these he will do, because I go to My Father. And whatever you ask in My name, that I will do, that the Father may be glorified in the Son. If you ask anything in My name, I will do it.

Not apostles, not prophets, but the ones who believe in Him will do the works that He did. The word *ask* in verses 13 and 14, may be accurately translated *demand.*[11] This is not to suggest that we demand of God, but rather we demand that the devil loose his hold on the person we are ministering to. Using the name of Jesus, we cast out the works of darkness.

God has granted you right standing with Himself. He has called you and prepared a place for you in His presence. The door to intimacy with the Father is opened. You have committed all to

---

[11] The Greek word is *aiteo*. In two of the most respected Greek authorities, the first definition given is *demand.* See Theological Dictionary of the New Testament, Vol. 1, p. 191; New International Dictionary of New Testament Theology, Volume 2, p. 855.

Him and have chosen to be a Father-Pleaser. He has authorized you to go and do the same works that Jesus did in His name.

-6-

DEEP AND INTIMATE KNOWLEDGE

Eph 1:17 AMP
For I always pray to the God of our Lord Jesus Christ, the
Father of glory, that He may grant you a spirit of wisdom
and revelation [of insight into mysteries and secrets] **in the
[deep and intimate] knowledge of Him...**

It is very possible for us to know many things about God and His
Word without it impacting the way we live. Intellectual
knowledge of God and His Word is desirable, but not necessarily
transforming in effect. Those whose hearts are hungry for more
of God can never be satisfied with mere intellectual knowledge
about God. They hunger for what some have called "heart
knowledge" of Him.

When Jesus said we would know the Truth and the Truth would
make us free, He clearly did not mean mental or intellectual
knowledge of the Truth. It seems clear that He implied that the
Truth should so take hold of us that it changes the way we live
our Christian life. In the Greek New Testament, there is a word
that describes the type of knowledge we are discussing:
epignosis. In Ephesians 1: 17, the Amplified Bible translates this
word *the deep and intimate knowledge* of God. W.E. Vine adds
that it means *full knowledge, a greater participation by the*

'knower' in the object 'known,' thus more powerfully influencing him. Thayer's Lexicon offers *precise and accurate* knowledge.

All of these definitions point us in the direction of a greater personal knowledge of our God Himself which results in changed lives. In the heart of every genuinely converted person is a desire to know God more intimately. In some cases a cloud of guilt and condemnation may obscure this desire, but as soon as the blood is applied to the deepest levels of the heart, this desire will reemerge. Our hearts long for God.

As we have been pointing out in this book, this longing is not only on Man's side. Our Father has created us for Himself and longs to walk in intimate fellowship with us. He has made every provision so that we can enter into this life of heart agreement with Him.

Our Desire

Free from guilt and shame, we find we desire to know our Father God intimately. It is especially important to recognize that He put that longing in us. We have been created for Him. Relationship comes before Rulership. You were created to reign through and for Him, but that dominion is a partnership with Him that flows out of intimate fellowship with Him. The first step into this intimate knowledge is to be hungry for it. If you do not find this hunger in your heart, ask the Father to help you resolve the unresolved issues in your life that hinder you from drinking from the well of longing for Him. He will help you.

Desire Released: Prayer

Our hunger needs to find expression. Prayer is a primary way to express our desire. Our Father, the Word says, will give us "the desires of our heart" (Ps. 37:4). This petition for the deep and intimate knowledge of God is expressed in other apostolic prayers of Paul, as well.

> **Colossians 1: 9-10**
> For this reason we also, since the day we heard it, do not cease to pray for you, and to ask that you may be **filled with the knowledge of His will** in all wisdom and spiritual understanding; that you may walk worthy of the Lord, fully pleasing Him, being fruitful in every good work and **increasing in the knowledge of God...**

Applying our word study to the first usage in this passage, we might say that we can pray for the precise and accurate knowledge of His will. Paul would not encourage us to ask for something that the Father is unwilling to give. Therefore, intimate knowledge of the will of God for our lives is available and offered. As we walk out the knowledge of His will we walk worthily of the Lord and become fruitful in good works. This results in an increasing *deep and intimate* knowledge of God Himself. Paul also mentions this full knowledge in his letter to the Philippians.

> **Philippians 1: 9**
> And this I pray, that your love may abound still more and more **in knowledge** and all discernment...

The word translated *abound* in the above verse means "to be present in super abundance." Paul is praying here that we would have a super abundance of the deep and intimate knowledge of God and the things of God. Why pray this for all the saints if Paul was not confident that his Father would, indeed, grant it?

Learning to Wait

One of the great challenges of my life was learning the discipline of consistent daily time with the Lord. This is a challenge for many. But let me assure you, God will help you if you ask Him to help. Getting quiet before the Lord and entering into His rest is a key to a deepening knowledge of Him. Learning to meditate in the Scriptures is a key to this type of knowledge. E.W. Kenyon calls it Revelation Knowledge. He refers to intellectual knowledge as Sense Knowledge or Mental Assent.

Father's desire is to reveal His Son. We come to know who the Father really is as we behold the Son in His glory. It is the Son's delight to reveal the Father to us.

Isaiah 40:31
But those **who wait on the Lord** shall renew their strength; they shall mount up with wings like eagles, they shall run and not be weary, they shall walk and not faint.

A key to daily renewal is learning to wait on the Lord. Learn to sit quietly in His presence with an expectant heart, not passively, but actively reaching out to Him with your inner man. Let the longing of your heart speak, rather than many words. As you quiet your mind and reach out from your heart, Father will impart to you or speak to you about the issues that are of real importance to your spiritual development. Sometimes not in words, but touching the deepest needs within us. The Hebrew word translated *wait* in the above verse, means *to wait with expectancy, to hope, to trust.* All these ideas are involved in our waiting upon the Lord. The word contains the idea of reaching out or grasping for something. We are reaching out to touch the Father's heart.

Impartation

The Word teaches that areas of Light that we walk in can be transferred to another by laying on of hands. Joshua had wisdom because Moses, who had the anointing of wisdom, laid his hands on Joshua. Many of us who have lacked the spiritual blessing of an earthly father can receive that missing blessing from a 'father' in the Lord. In like manner those who are walking in a revelation of the Father's heart can, as the Lord wills, pass it on to others. Paul, as he contemplated visiting Rome, expressed a similar desire.

Romans 1:11
For I long to see you, that I may **impart** to you some spiritual gift, so that you may be established.

Paul understood that he could release gifts and blessings to those he laid his hands on. In his letter to Timothy, he reminded him to "stir up the gift of God which is in you **through the laying on of my hands**" (2 Tim. 1:6).

There are many in the Body of Christ who can impart the Father's blessing. We can ask them to lay hands on us and impart this blessing to us. If we are hungry, the Lord will bring us into this unfolding revelation one way or another.

Matthew 5:6
Blessed are those who hunger and thirst for righteousness, for they shall be filled.

If what I have written thus far has stirred a hunger within you, know that it is the Holy Spirit working and He stirs our hunger so He can also satisfy that hunger.

-7-

THE LIVING WORD

There are only two ways we develop our intimacy with the Father: Through Prayer and the Word. Time spent alone with God is essential to foster this deep, rich Fellowship. But we must also recognize that we meet the Father and He is unveiled to us in the revelation of Scripture. The Bible is the only 100% reliable standard for judging our religious experiences. What the Word says about our Father is always the pure Truth and it never changes.

When our Fellowship is weak, the Word will sometimes condemn us. This is not the Father's intention, but simply what happens when our sin-conscious minds interpret the Word. As we grow in faith, we shed the nagging sense of sin and come instead to be son-conscious. Welcome in the presence of our Father, we refuse condemnation and cast down the accuser of the brethren.

Resting in Him

When we start to rest in what Christ has done for us in His Finished Work, and no longer try to attain anything by our own works, the Word begins to open up to us marvelously. We are coming to know the grace of God in truth.

65

Colossians 1:5-6

...because of the hope which is laid up for you in heaven, of which you heard before in the word of the truth of the gospel, which has come to you, as it has also in all the world, and is bringing forth fruit, as it is also among you **since the day you heard and knew the grace of God in truth**.

As we come to know and understand the grace of God in Reality, the Word's supernatural ability begins to work in us. The Word brings forth after it's own kind. Incorruptible Seed brings forth incorruptible fruit. His Word works in us to form Christ in us.

The Spirit of wisdom and revelation in the deep and intimate knowledge of Him begins to flood the eyes of our understanding with Light. We begin to perceive the glorious hope to which we are called. Father begins to reveal the exceedingly great power that works in us as believers (Eph. 1:17-23).

The Old Covenant used many different names for the one, true God. Each name revealed a facet of the Divine Nature. All these names tell us something profound about our Father God. But Jesus had a favorite name for His Father: *Father!* Jesus dared to call the God of the Jews His Father and the Pharisees wanted to kill Him for doing it. But Jesus, as a Son, was the only One who could truly reveal the God of the Old Covenant. The Jews knew Him in part, but Jesus revealed His fullness. Jesus was the exact representation of His Person, the Brightness of His Glory (Heb. 1:3).

The Father is Fully Revealed in Christ

We must be careful not to allow the partial and incomplete revelation of God in the Old Covenant to in any way color the perfect, full revelation of the Father in Jesus Christ. He is the will of the Father in manifestation. He manifested constantly the mercy of His Father. The only people He was angry with were the religious leaders whose teaching obscured rather than revealed His Father. He was rich in mercy toward all others and healed all their sick. And He is the same Yesterday, Today and Forever (Heb. 13:8).

Jesus is the Word revealed. He said His Words are Spirit and they are Life. It is the Father's intention as you read the written Word to unveil the Living Word to you. He who is the perfect unveiling of the Father, with Whom there is no variation or shadow of turning, is He who only gives good gifts (James 1:17). When we read the written Word in the Light of this clear revelation of the Father in the Son, we start to meet the Father and the Son every time we open the written Word. The Personality behind the written Word bleeds through to us and we receive fresh revelation of our God. We begin to love the written Word like we do the Living Word, because He meets us in its pages. The promises become our source for partaking of the Divine Nature (2 Pet. 1:4).

The Father has already given Jesus a "Yes and Amen" to all His promises. And as His joint-heirs, we have access to all the promises of God as well.

2 Corinthians 1:20

For all the promises of God in Him are Yes, and in Him Amen, to the glory of God through us.

Daring to Believe

If we are honest, many times we struggle to actually accept what the Word says to us, and to take it personally. Notice what Jesus said in His Upper Room Discourse:

John 16:26-27

In that day you will ask in My name, and I do not say to you that I shall pray the Father for you; for **the Father Himself loves you**, because you have loved Me, and have believed that I came forth from God.

Because we have loved the One who died for us, the Father loves us. Not because of our works or perfect obedience, but rather because we believe Jesus came forth from the Father. As our faith grows, so does our experience of the Father's love. We dare to believe that the Father is so satisfied by what Jesus accomplished that our acceptance is forever settled. We are welcome in His presence because we are accepted in the Beloved (Eph. 1:6).

-8-

ABIDING

John 14:2-3
In My Father's house are many mansions; if it were not so, I would have told you. I go to prepare a place for you. And if I go and prepare a place for you, I will come again and receive you to Myself; that where I am, there you may be also.

In this familiar verse, many believe Jesus is describing our heavenly mansion. I am sure that our eternal dwelling place in heaven will be a glorious reality, beyond what we could ask or think. I want, however, to suggest another possible (and very likely) interpretation. Notice this more literal translation of the verse:

John 14:2, 3 Recovery Version
In My Father's House are many abodes; if it were not so, I would have told you; for I go to prepare a place for you. And if I go and prepare a place for you, I am coming again and will receive you to Myself, so that where I am you also may be.

The word translated *mansions* in our versions is translated *abodes* in this version. It means a dwelling place. It is only used one other time in the New Testament, in John 14:23.

John 14: 23 Recovery Version

Jesus answered and said to him, "If anyone loves Me, he will keep My word; and My Father will love him, and We will come to him and make an abode with him.

I point this out to suggest John isn't talking about heaven when we die, but rather our union with Christ after the Day of Pentecost. The word translated *abode* is the noun form of the word translated *abide* in chapter fifteen. If we were reading Greek we would easily see the connection.

John 15:5

I am the vine, you are the branches. He who abides in Me, and I in him, bears much fruit; for without Me you can do nothing.

Jesus went to prepare an abiding place for us enthroned with Him at the Father's right hand. This was later revealed to the apostle Paul and he stated it this way:

Ephesians 2:5-7

...even when we were dead in trespasses, made us alive together with Christ (by grace you have been saved), and raised us up together, and **made us sit together in the heavenly places** in Christ Jesus, that in the ages to come He might show the exceeding riches of His grace in His kindness toward us in Christ Jesus.

Jesus prepared a place for us in Him, where we identify with Him in His death, burial, resurrection and are enthroned at the Father's right hand, *that where He is we may be also.* Not in the next life, but now in Christ. As our apprehension of His Finished Work grows, we enter into the Rest of Faith. We cease trying to earn God's approval, and believe that Jesus did all that is necessary to satisfy the Father and make us totally acceptable in Him.

As we press on to know the Lord, we cease from our striving and are filled with praise and thanksgiving for what He has already done for us. As the Holy Spirit reveals to us all that is ours as joint-heirs with Christ, we find ourselves resting in Him – abiding in Him. We no longer see ourselves separate from Him, but we see ourselves *in Him*.

1 Corinthians 6:17
But he who is joined to the Lord is one spirit with Him.

I now see myself united with Christ in a union of spirit-made Reality by my Father when He placed me in Christ. The Holy Spirit bears joint-testimony that I am truly born of God. Not just legally, but vitally – experientially. As I, by faith, thank the Father for what He says He has done the Holy Spirit witnesses with my spirit that it is Truth. My assurance grows and I am filled with thanksgiving and praise. I am overwhelmed by His goodness and grace.

1 Cor 1:30 NASU
But by His doing you are in Christ Jesus, who became to us wisdom from God, and righteousness and sanctification, and redemption.

It was out of the Father's great desire that you are in Christ. His desire for Relationship and Fellowship compelled Him to draw us to Christ and reveal Him to us. At our point of faith we left our position in Adam and were joined in spirit to Christ. *By His doing we are in Christ.* We passed from spiritual death in Adam to spiritual Life in Christ. Old things passed away, and behold, all things became new. And all things are of God (2 Cor. 5:17, 18).

Father wants us to learn to abide – settle down, dwell – in union with Christ. The Holy Spirit is in us to teach us how to enter into this Reality. It belongs to every believer and is part of the abundance of grace freely given us in Christ. In the simplicity of child-like faith we receive from the inexhaustible riches of His grace. Receive it by faith and trust the Holy Spirit to make it real to your inner man.

Cease From Your Own Works

One of the greatest challenges in our walk with God is to stop striving and just believe. Everything Christ has provided through His death, burial, resurrection and enthroning is now ours in Christ. Father wants us to receive what Jesus has provided, but He cannot honor any attempts to earn it by our works. Our works create self-righteousness. His work creates true Righteousness. Righteousness is a gift of grace freely given us in Christ.

Hebrews 4:1-3
Therefore, since a promise remains of entering His rest, let us fear lest any of you seem to have come short of it. For indeed

the gospel was preached to us as well as to them; but the word which they heard did not profit them, not being mixed with faith in those who heard it. For we who have believed do enter that rest, as He has said: "So I swore in My wrath, 'they shall not enter My rest,'" although the works were finished from the foundation of the world.

A few verses later in Hebrews it states:

Hebrews 4:10
For he who has entered His rest has himself also ceased from his works as God did from His.

What joy can be ours when we realize our Father has already met our every need in Christ! Rather than mourning our inadequacies we celebrate His perfect provision. We find ourselves 'being confident of this very thing, that He who has begun a good work in you will complete it until the day of Jesus Christ' Philippians 1:6.

Rather than having a highly developed faith in our inadequacies, we begin to rejoice in His complete faithfulness, His perfect provision, and the ability of the indwelling Spirit to guide us into all the Finished Work of Christ. We trade our destructive unbelief for a living Faith in an absolutely perfect Savior who is able to save, heal and deliver to the uttermost those who draw near to God through Him (Heb. 7:25).

Abiding and Freedom

John 8:31-32

Then Jesus said to those Jews who believed Him, "If you abide in My word, you are My disciples indeed. And you shall know the truth, and the truth shall make you free."

We often hear verse 32 quoted out of context. Freedom is promised to those who learn to rest and live in the Word of God. As we seek the Lord to open these Truths to us they become more real than our feelings or perceptions. Father's Truth becomes our Truth and the Holy Spirit bears witness with our spirit that we are truly born of God.

In the American Standard Version of Luke 1:37 it says, "No Word from God shall be void of power." Our hearts were designed to be good ground in which the Incorruptible Seed of God's Word can take root and grow. As the Spirit unveils these riches to us our faith grows exceedingly. Fears, condemnation and shame find no place in our consciousness. Instead of being sin-conscious we become son-conscious. Our sense of belonging in the Family of the Father grows by leaps and bounds. Our joy increases as never before.

Abiding and Dominion

We were created for dominion. We are to rule over the enemies of the Kingdom of God, releasing Kingdom Realities in the earth. As we learn to abide in Him we intelligently partner with Him in releasing His authority.

John 15:7 Author's Literal Translation

If you abide in Me, and My Word abides in you, you will demand what you determine and it will come into being.

If we are abiding in Him, and His Word has become our abiding place as well, we can partner with Him in commanding the works of darkness to bow to the Name of Jesus on our lips. Our lives can become exceedingly fruitful to the glory of God the Father. It doesn't matter what your previous experiences have been, the Truth can make you free.

Philippians 3:13-14

Brethren, I do not count myself to have apprehended; but one thing I do, forgetting those things which are behind and reaching forward to those things which are ahead, I press toward the goal for the prize of the upward call of God in Christ Jesus.

-9-

THE THREE WITNESSES

There is no division in the Godhead. The Father, Son and Spirit are united in their desire to see mankind back in the Relationship and Fellowship they desired from eternity past. Paul tells us that

> Eph 1:4-6 CJB
> In the Messiah he chose us in love before the creation of the universe to be holy and without defect in his presence. He determined in advance that through Yeshua the Messiah we would be his sons - in keeping with his pleasure and purpose - so that we would bring him praise commensurate with the glory of the grace he gave us through the Beloved One.

Father chose us in Christ before the foundation of the world to be holy and without defect in His presence. This is His purpose and our destiny. We are His workmanship – His work of Art – recreated in Christ Jesus for good works that our Father planned beforehand for us to walk in (see Eph. 2:10).

Much of the teaching in the Body of Christ today, well meaning though it is, does not help us come into the intimacy with the Father that produces lasting change. Rather, it focuses us on our weaknesses and shortcomings with the hope of bringing conviction and repentance. The intention is good, but the methodology is misguided. True repentance (which is a change in the way we think, not a feeling of sorrow over our sinfulness) comes as a result of Father bestowing more grace upon us. It is the goodness (or kindness) of God that leads to repentance.

Every time the Word brings you new Light on the grace and goodness of God, you adjust your thinking to agree with heaven. That is repentance. As our hearts are touched by the Father's love, we want to forsake the carnal attitudes and activities that we may have previously tolerated. We want to please our loving heavenly Father. His unconditional Love flowing into us in our weakness works lasting change in us. We become hungry for more of the deep and intimate knowledge of Him and His will. We desire to walk worthily of Him, fully pleasing Him and increasing in this deep and intimate knowledge of our gracious Father (see Col. 1:9, 10).

God the Father is For Us

Rom 8:31-33 YLT

What, then, shall we say unto these things? if God is for us, who is against us? He who indeed His own Son did not spare, but for us all did deliver him up, how shall He not also with him the all things grant to us? Who shall lay a charge against the choice ones of God? God is He that is declaring righteous...

Who shall lay a charge against the choice ones of God? You are a choice one! God has declared you righteous. If God the Father is for us, who is against us? The ultimate authority and Judge of all the earth is on record as being for you. Dare you accept it? He has declared you righteous. Will you argue with Him about your unworthiness? Receive the grace of God and rejoice, don't question Him in unbelief. Faith pleases God. Father is for you, none can be against you.

God the Son is For Us

Romans 8:34-35

Who is he who condemns? It is Christ who died, and furthermore is also risen, who is even at the right hand of God, who also makes intercession for us. Who shall separate us from the love of Christ?

Note that our Father rebukes those who would bring a charge against us. Here the Son stands with us against all condemnation. He also prays for us that we might fully appropriate the grace necessary to overcome fleshly weaknesses. Without any condemnation!

The Father and Son agree that we should be free from accusation and condemnation. Let's agree with them and receive this amazing grace.

God the Spirit is For Us

We have looked at the testimony of the Father and the Son in regard to our freedom from condemnation and shame. Now let's consider what the Holy Spirit testifies in this arena. In the book of Hebrews the great superiority of the New Covenant is being expounded. The once-and-for-all sacrifice of Christ is shown to be the answer to the needs of mankind. Jeremiah's prophecy of the New Covenant is quoted with this amazing statement:

Hebrews 10:15-18
But the Holy Spirit also witnesses to us; for after He had said before, 'This is the covenant that I will make with them after those days, says the Lord: I will put My laws into their hearts, and in their minds I will write them,' then He adds, '**Their sins and their lawless deeds I will remember no more.**' Now where there is remission of these, there is no longer an offering for sin.

Here the Holy Spirit witnesses (or testifies) to us that Father will remember our sins and lawless deeds no more! What good news! You and I are people without a past. The blood of Christ has cleansed away every stain of past failure. All of this so we can stand unashamed in His presence.

If God is For Us

The Triune God is in agreement that we should be free from guilt, shame and condemnation. He has made a perfect provision for us when we step out of the Light into the Darkness. If we confess our sins He is Faithful and Righteous to forgive us our sins and cleanse us from all unrighteousness (1John 1:9). Forgiven and cleansed not because we deserve it, but rather because He is faithful to the perfect sacrifice of Christ and Righteous as the Covenant-keeping God.

Isaiah 44:22

I have blotted out, like a thick cloud, your transgressions, and like a cloud, your sins. Return to Me, for I have redeemed you.

Here, even in the Old Covenant, we see the Father's heart to restore and bring back into fellowship with Himself His Covenant people. How much more in the New Covenant with its better promises, better High Priest and better Sacrifice is provision made for restoring fellowship. In his letter to the Colossians (Col. 2:6), he talks of our being established in our faith and overflowing in it with thanksgiving. As we come to comprehend the amazing grace of God given us in Christ we cannot help but overflow with gratitude and worship. He is worthy of all our praise.

In the early days of my walk with the Lord I constantly stumbled in an area of sin. I would come back to the Father riddled with shame and grief. One day I was asking forgiveness and feeling quite unworthy. As I confessed my sin and asked for forgiveness, the Father spoke to me: "Son, I require nothing of you but what flows out of your relationship with Me."

I came to understand that my Father had the answers to my struggles and eventually He led me to a complete deliverance. It took some time, but I learned that my Father was my ally in my fight against sin. There was no condemnation in His heart for me even when I fell. This truth alone was significant in gaining lasting victory.

Hebrews 4:14-16

Seeing then that we have a great High Priest who has passed through the heavens, Jesus the Son of God, let us hold fast our confession. For we do not have a High Priest who cannot sympathize with our weaknesses, but was in all points tempted as we are, yet without sin. Let us therefore come boldly to the throne of grace, that we may obtain mercy and find grace to help in time of need.

FINAL THOUGHTS

You have read the book. Have you seen a glimpse of your heavenly Father that has stirred a desire in your heart for greater intimacy with Him? That is the intent of this book. This writing may have challenged long-held ideas about the God of the Bible. But let me encourage you to carefully note the scriptures quoted in the book. Look at them in their context and see that none are saying something different than I have implied. Satisfy your mind as to the biblical accuracy of what has been taught. Once satisfied, seek the Father with all your heart, and you will find Him.

Jeremiah 29:13

And you will seek Me and find Me, when you search for Me with all your heart.

Books by Joe McIntyre:

E.W. Kenyon and His Message of Faith: The True Story
Ever wonder what the true roots of the Faith Message were? This book allows E.W. Kenyon, from previously unpublished writings, to answer his critics. Kenyon tells who really influenced him (and who he was opposed to all of his life: the metaphysical cults). This book documents the rich Evangelical history of 19th Century divine healing in what was known as the "Faith-Cure" movement.

Who We Are in Christ (Book or CD)
Ever struggle with your identity and sense of worth? Knowing what God has done for you in the Finished Work of Christ will set you free from double-mindedness and establish you in the grace of God. You are a New Creation, the Workmanship of God. God has given you His Righteousness so you can stand in His presence without condemnation. This book is an exposition of these life-changing Truths.

Kingdom Warriors (Book or CD)
Rick Joyner, in his *Final Quest* book, relates a vision in which a horde of demonic forces attack the Church. Many believers cave in to these forces, Joyner points out, because they did not have on their armor. This book is an in-depth look at the armor with practical ways to implement it in daily life. These Truths were personally life-changing for the author.

War Over the Word (Book or CD)
As a believer in Jesus you have been enlisted into the drama of the conflict of the ages. God has made every provision for us to overcome the Adversary and all the adversity he sends our way. Christ's Finished Work perfectly meets the needs of every believer in every circumstance. The provision is in the promise. All the promises of God are Yes and Amen in Christ. We are His joint-heirs.

Other available CD series by Joe McIntyre:

Our Righteousness in Christ

Our Identification with Christ

Blood Covenant

The Word of His Grace

Throne Life

To order Books or CDs, please visit our website:

www.thehealingcentre.us
or call us - 425.424.3801.

Word of His Grace Church & Ministry Center
18706 North Creek Pkwy Suite104 Bothell, WA 98011